**A Measurement of Annual GDP Performance of the 162 WTO Members Between**

**1989-2001 and 2002-2014.**

Alan Bayham BA, MS

CHS, ASU, and UofP

Phoenix, Arizona USA

©2016

## Abstract

*The annual GDP performance mean between all 162 World Trade Organization countries was measured between two time periods: 1989-2001 and 2002 and 2014. The 10 best and worst performing nations were measured and analyzed against each other for each time period. The 10 nations with the largest positive and negative annual GDP mean performance shift was compiled and discussed. Discussion regarding the data, WTO membership, and external trade networks is included, and the article incorporates an analysis effective austerity measures, lack of diversification, and membership in trade and political organizations, which have led to both positive and negative outcomes in relation to annual GDP mean economic performance for WTO member nations over the two time periods measured. Analysis regarding the annual GDP mean performance concludes that the WTO has promoted world trade throughout the world, and this has directly resulted in an increase of annual GDP mean performance by 29% over the two time periods studied for WTO member nations.*

Keywords: world, trade, organization, gross, domestic, product, economics

<u>Information</u>

## Gross Domestic Product

The gross domestic product of a nation is used by economists as one of the primary economic indicators to measure the strength and health of countries economies (Investopedia, 2016). The GDP represents the total monetary value of all goods and services produced by a nation over a period of time, and it should be thought of as a representation of the size of a country's economy. Economists arrive at the figure of a country's GSP in one of two ways: by adding up the annual income of a nation or by adding up the money spent within a nation. The income approach is calculated by adding up employees salaries, gross profits of companies within a nation, and taxes minus subsidies. The expenditure method, which is considered to be more common, is calculated by adding a nation's total consumption, investments, government spending, and net exports. A country's GDP figures, which show a nation's economic production and growth, impacts everyone within an economy because it reflects a country's economic health. Significant changes in a nation's GDP has a large impact on its unemployment rate, wage increases, and stock markets. Thus, poor GDP figures result in weakened economic growth for a nation, which results in fewer jobs, fewer profits, and lower stock prices. Negative GDP growth is what investors use to determine the strength of a nation's economy and whether or not it has entered an economic recession.

## The World Trade Organization

The World Trade Organization was developed in 1995 from the General Agreement on Tariffs and Trade in 1947 (Heakal, 2016). The goal of GATT was to reduce tariffs and facilitate the global trade of goods following WWII, and it was based on the Most Favored Nation clause that allowed selected countries privileged trading rights within specific national economies. The goal of GATT was to increase competition between nations by permitting them to have equal trading rights, so individual nations would not have trading advantages over others. From 1947 to 1994, the trading regulations established through GATT governed multilateral trading between participating nations, and it worked to address agricultural issues and anti-dumping regulations between its members as well. The Uruguay round is of particular importance in the history of GATT because it laid the framework for a general agreement on trade for services, and it established regulations to protect intellectual property rights within nations.

Neither GATT nor the WTO have made public a list of definitive governing rules between member nations, but there is a consensus among most economists that the organization should be rules-based (Baldwin, 2016). The five governing principles agreed upon by most economists that should be interpreted as constitutional are as follows: nondiscrimination, transparency, reciprocity, flexibility, and consensus in decision-making. Nondiscrimination refers to the lack of favoritism that can be displayed toward member nations, transparency refers to the reduction of conflicts regarding trade when policies are made public, reciprocity refers to what nations can expect from other nations when they remove national trade barriers, flexibility refers to permittance of nations to use tariffs against member nations in order to maintain domestically significant industries, and consensus refers to decision-making processes in which agreements are made regarding regulations by member nations.

The goal of the WTO is to ensure that global trade functions in free and predictable manner, and, as a result of establishing ground rules for global trade within member nations, it has laid the legal framework for a system of international commerce between the majority of nations embodying the planet (Heakal, 2016). The stated purpose of the organization is "economic peace and stability in the world through a multilateral system based on consenting member states", and the organization currently has 162 member nations who have consented to the regulations and upheld ordinances from the organization at the national level (Heakal, 2016, p. 1). This means that the WTO's regulations are adopted and become part of a national framework of legislation that is wholly adopted by a member nation's domestic legal system. The regulations outlined in the agreement of member nations are applied at the national level to local and national companies when conducting international business, and these regulations extend to national companies that set up organizations in other countries throughout the world.

Decisions regarding the regulations imposed by the WTO are generally made by a consensus, but a majority vote is periodically used (Heakal, 2016). The Ministerial Committee is based in Geneva, Switzerland, and it holds meetings to make top decisions at least every two years. There are also a number of councils and committees working to ensure freer trade within the organization. The WTO resolves disputes between nations in regards to trade barriers placed on particular goods, and, if a resolution does not occur following negotiations, the organization can issue trade sanctions against nations in violation of their regulations.

## Criticisms of the WTO

The WTO has been the target of protests around the world because individuals within member nations feel that the multilateral trading systems have led to policies that are undemocratic and result in a lack of transparency during negotiations of the Ministerial Committee (Heakal, 2016). Critics also believe that nations who are members of the WTO compromise national sovereignty because the organization functions as a global authority on trade and constantly has the right to review a member nation's domestic trade policies. Member countries often have to sacrifice national interests to maintain membership in the WTO and not to violate agreements, which limits a nation's choices and ability to protect key industries within its domestic market. Opponents also note that democratic countries may continue to do business with totalitarian regimes in the name of free trade as a result of the WTO, and they feel that these instances, specifically when democratic governments continue to conduct trade with nondemocratic governments, that big business is favored over human rights and individuals' right to freedom.

Other instances that have alarmed critics of the WTO's regulations are in relation to intellectual property, and it has sparked debate surrounding human rights (Heakal, 2016). A well-known instance is in regards to the patenting of medicines in which national governments in both sub-Saharan Africa and South America forbid the manufacture of generic drugs that are needed by the poor to save lives because they do not want to violate ordinances set forth by the WTO and comprise their nation's membership. The reality is that individuals in many of these nations are in need of these drugs, but they simply cannot afford the non-generic versions of them. They, however, are left to die by the WTO and their governments to avoid possible trade sanctions resulting from violations of intellectual property imposed through the organization's regulations.

Membership in the WTO typically benefits member nations and can facilitate investment in nations, which can assist in boosting national economies and increase the standard of living for all participating nations (Heakal, 2016). Investors from developed economies have historically been at an advantage over nations with less wealth, and this results in a cycle in which investors developed economies end up having great influence over poorer nations. These regulations, however, are in investors' interest and can help facilitate an investment process that would not exist on such a large scale without the WTO, but it is clear that controversy surrounding free trade and freedom will continue to persist well into the future as the WTO continues to grow in conjunction with the continued evolution of the global economic system it has helped to create.

## Benefits of the WTO to Member Nations

Theoretically, members of the WTO should have equal access to each other's markets, and no nation should have superiority over other members of the organization in relation to trade (Beattie, 2016). This, however, does not happen in practice in consideration of the system of tariff brokering in which nations are permitted to protect vital national industries if the removal of tariffs would lead to the loss of crucial national industries. Presently, WTO members nations are permitted to add most industries considered to be of national importance, and developed nations are attempting to presently add the effects of lost labor and lack of production to this list to justify an increase in tariffs.

In general, tariffs are taxes imposed on purchases of specific products in most nations, and they result in increasing government revenue and, potentially, have negative side effects for consumers (Beattie, 2016). When tariffs are imposed on a product, foreign products cost more at the domestic level, and national manufacturers often raise their prices as well to increase profits. This unfortunately results in higher prices being paid by consumers and less competition in domestics markets, and the result is often national governments use public money from tariffs to produce and support inferior products. Ultimately, WTO-sanctioned tariffs, anti-dumping measures, and restrictive quotas used to protect national industries end up hurting national industries because they do not expose them to international competition, which results in the removal of necessary competition needed to invest in new technologies, control costs, and improve production. This essentially results in international competitors becoming more innovative and stronger, which makes national core industries increasingly vulnerable to true free trade and forces consumers to pay premium prices for domestic goods. Domestic consumers are typically unaware of these taxes because they take the form of stealth tariffs, and this results in increasing governments revenue at the expense of the consumer to make foreign products less competitive in comparison to lower quality national products through hidden and smaller taxes than most citizens are used to.

## WTO Transparency

One of the main criticisms of the WTO is the lack of transparency it has during its meetings, which contradicts one of the main objectives that it set for itself when the organization was GATT (Beattie, 2016). In settling disputes or developing new regulations, it has regularly been unclear which nations were involved in the decision making process. Liberals view this lack of transparency as the result of committees made up of economically stronger nations within the WTO conspiring to exploit less developed and economically weaker nations. This view appears to be true because historically the most economically powerful nations set the WTO's agenda, and they were the first to endorse anti-dumping acts to protect domestically vital industries. Free market supporters have attacked the WTO policymaking process on the grounds that the organization has increasingly made free trade heavily politicized and complicated. They argue that if free trade were to exist between nations that the organization would be completely unneeded and that to properly encourage trade governments would permit private companies to trade on a deal-by-deal basis with no international oversight.

## The Evolution of the WTO

The WTO started with 23 member nations in 1947, but it has grown to 162 members nations today that have universally accepted and follow the regulations set forth by the organization (Baldwin, 2016). For most imports among these nations, tariffs imposed are below 5%, but there are no tariffs for a large share of the imports among member nations. Since 2001, there have been 20 nations that have joined the WTO, which includes both China and Russia. Over the last 15 years, the majority of WTO members have substantially lowered trade barriers among member nations, but, depending on how it is viewed, these tariffs, fortunately or unfortunately, have been made bilaterally, regionally, and unilaterally, which has effectively diminished the power of the WTO and the trade agreements through it between nations.

As a result of the weakening of the WTO through alternative trade negotiations between nations and regions, there has been little progress on the liberalization of trade for over the last two decades, and, in some ways, the implications of both multilateral and regional trade talks has minimized the effectiveness and power of GATT as the WTO (Baldwin, 2016). The WTO has dramatically shifted power since its inception from the Quad to the emerging economies who have taken up membership. This has been a significant development and reflects a dramatic shift in power from the Quad, which are developed economies, to the emerging markets throughout the world. The Quad used to account for 75% of the world's imports, but, over the last two decades, this has changed to 50% of the world's imports. The result is a weakening of negotiation power during trade talks for developed nations because of the power adjustment and the subsequent wealth transfer to the developing economies throughout the world. This power shift has resulted from coalitions between developing nations, and it has resulted in increased economic and blocking-power by them in negotiations with the Quad, which has permitted them to effectively block efforts by developed economies to enter into politically sensitive domestic markets. Thus, it has undermined in many ways the original principals set forth in GATT and adopted by the WTO because the addition of more member nations to the organization has not lead to increased demand and better access to markets for all member nations, especially developed nations.

The WTO stands as a pillar of multilateral economic governance today, similar to GATT, despite superlative trade agreements made bilaterally, regionally, and unilaterally (Baldwin, 2016). The WTO still oversees universal norms of rule-based trade for all 162 participating nations, and it still settles trade disputes between member nations and issues regulations that are followed by nearly all its members. It, however, has not updated its rules since 1994, and it has failed to adopt to the growth of businesses and the adoption of the Internet for business by most business worldwide in the twenty-first century. Although no new regulations have been set by the WTO for over 20 years, there have been substantial regional trade agreements between advanced and developing economies and continued tariff cutting, and there has been over 3,000 bilateral international investment treaties signed to date. Thus, global trade and rule writing have continued over the last two decades, but they have circumvented both the regulations and regulatory processes set forth by the WTO.

The regional agreements, tariff cutting, and bilateral investment treaties conducted outside of the WTO has kept the level of free trade high (Baldwin, 2016). Trade diversion, resulting from bilateral and regional trade agreements, has shown little economic evidence that has impacted the world economy a great deal, and, in instances were tariffs remain high, these trade deals have a tendency to exclude sensitive items as a result of these regional trade agreements, which has resulted in few preferences created that negatively impacting the WTO's outdated rules. Although there has been little impact on the WTO's antiquated regulations to date, most economists feel that the future of megaregional agreements, like the Trans-Pacific Partnership and the Trans-Atlantic Trade and Investment Partnership, present a threat to the present status quo of international trade regulations governed by the WTO. They feel that this will result in an international trading system that is fragmented, and it will ultimately exclude nations that are not partners, like China and India. It will most likely end up weakening the WTO, and it will result in a second pillar of systems that circumvent the WTO and weaken its power over free trade on goods and services, investment and intellectual property regulation, and the movement of personnel by multinational organizations. This will most likely have a domino effect throughout regions and indirectly impact all 162 nations that are currently part of the WTO who will follow the larger economies trade models that are looking to adopt regional protectionism for national interests against fast growing developing economies, like China and India.

## Purpose, Rationale, and Hypothesis

The purpose of this study was to investigate WTO member nations over two periods: 1989 to 2001 and 2002 to 2014. The rationale for choosing to measure WTO member nations GDPs is based in economic theory because it is used by economists worldwide in measuring the strength and performance of economies. Therefore, to measure the strength and performance of WTO member nations, the annual GDP mean performance was used for the two aforementioned periods of time and measured against each other. The periods selected represent the annual GDP mean performance of the present 162 members previous to China's entrance to the WTO and thereafter. This is substantial because China is presently the one of the world's largest, the most populated country in the world, and, in many ways, represents a shift in power from the United States, the European Union, Japan, and Canada or the Quad to developing economies throughout the world. This is an investigation on whether or not the effects of joining the WTO has been beneficial for both developed and developing economies, and it will analyze and compare the best and worst annual GDP mean performance by all member nations over the two periods of time mentioned above. It will also investigate the effect of increased free trade on the newer member nations of the WTO in comparison to longtime members of the organization. It is hypothesized that the increased free trade and membership in the WTO have been beneficial for the developing economies and has negatively impacted the developed economies throughout the world who are members of the WTO.

**Methods**

The study was conducted by retrieving annual growth from all countries who were members of WTO in 2014 for two periods of time: 1989 to 2001 and 2002 to 2014. Member nations annual GDP mean performance data was recovered from both comparative periods from the World Bank's website, and current membership information was recovered and verified from the WTO's website. Because of the political situation and size of the market, nations that are members of the European Union and the EU are considered separately by both the World Bank and the WTO, so they are done so as well in this study.

Data from annual GDP mean performance was categorically compiled for each year and separated into the two periods being studied, and the mean for each period was calculated as well as the mean for all nations per time period. The raw data includes GDP performance for all present members of the WTO, but the data compiled did not distinguish between GDP performance in accordance with the date of membership. This was done intentionally for comparative purposes. Member nations that failed to report GDP data for any given year of the time periods were excluded from the performance data to maintain the integrity of the statistical data and the investigation.

Finally, the 10 best and worst performing nations were extracted from each time period tested. There performance was then measured against the opposing time period tested, and a percentage of performance increase or loss was factored individually as well as the mean performance gain or loss for each group. Also, the 10 nations with the largest positive and negative annual GDP mean performance shift was compiled, investigated, and discussed.

**Results**

The gross domestic product annual mean for all countries who were world trade organization members by 2016 was calculated individually from 1989 to 2001 and, then, averaged. An average for all member nation was also calculated to derive a base mean for WTO's members performance for this period, and member nations that failed to report annual GDP data for each established time frame analyzed were not included in this research. All nations included in this analysis reported national annual GDP data to

the World Bank in 12 out of the 12 years studied. The average GDP mean for all
member nations from the years 1989 to 2001 was 3.10.

| Country Name | GDP Mean 1989-2001 |
|---|---|
| Albania | 2.311617942 |
| Angola | 1.352123317 |
| Antigua and Barbuda | 3.134286381 |
| Argentina | 2.501374337 |
| Armenia | *not enough data* |
| Australia | 3.272611315 |
| Austria | 2.756691749 |
| Bahrain | 4.873541092 |
| Bangladesh | 4.641561628 |
| Barbados | 0.798559926 |
| Belgium | 2.300586939 |
| Belize | 6.836949903 |
| Benin | 4.44300709 |
| Bolivia | 3.685936611 |
| Botswana | 5.328176416 |
| Brazil | 2.139919138 |
| Brunei Darussalam | 1.949438381 |
| Bulgaria | -1.329080131 |
| Burkina Faso | 4.755378365 |
| Burundi | -0.906530597 |
| Cabo Verde | 9.504301006 |
| Cambodia | *not enough data* |
| Cameroon | 0.869067276 |
| Canada | 2.539873857 |
| Central African Republic | 1.297202206 |
| Chad | 2.909345526 |
| Chile | 6.320067352 |
| China | 9.311780299 |
| Colombia | 2.932544795 |
| Congo, Dem. Rep. | -4.997698797 |
| Congo, Rep. | 1.716874318 |
| Costa Rica | 4.824672024 |
| Cote d'Ivoire | 1.958998992 |
| Croatia | *not enough data* |

| | |
|---|---|
| Cuba | -0.782850534 |
| Cyprus | 4.711197845 |
| Czech Republic | *not enough data* |
| Denmark | 2.296494483 |
| Djibouti | *not enough data* |
| Dominica | 1.799723482 |
| Dominican Republic | 4.750037102 |
| Ecuador | 2.251503827 |
| Egypt, Arab Rep. | 4.402023761 |
| El Salvador | 4.133946872 |
| Estonia | *not enough data* |
| Fiji | 3.028358746 |
| Finland | 2.456558114 |
| France | 2.32631411 |
| Gabon | 2.58107361 |
| Gambia, The | 3.716320604 |
| Georgia | -6.980494665 |
| Germany | 2.362603226 |
| Ghana | 4.264427823 |
| Greece | 2.497079815 |
| Grenada | 3.155316376 |
| Guatemala | 3.888851239 |
| Guinea | 3.930348983 |
| Guinea-Bissau | 2.057034761 |
| Guyana | 3.369386179 |
| Haiti | *not enough data* |
| Honduras | 3.104705697 |
| Hong Kong SAR, China | 3.604751076 |
| Hungary | *not enough data* |
| Iceland | 2.44131016 |
| India | 5.561437644 |
| Indonesia | 5.076590863 |
| Ireland | 7.216977262 |
| Israel | 5.194818351 |
| Italy | 1.824300893 |
| Jamaica | 2.384664038 |
| Japan | 1.744543148 |
| Jordan | 3.469609584 |
| Kazakhstan | *not enough data* |

| | |
|---|---|
| Kenya | 2.423876636 |
| Korea, Rep. | 6.683490592 |
| Kuwait | *not enough data* |
| Kyrgyz Republic | -1.591536826 |
| Lao PDR | 6.806081578 |
| Latvia | *not enough data* |
| Lesotho | 4.13611013 |
| Liechtenstein | 4.924449166 |
| Lithuania | *not enough data* |
| Luxembourg | 5.230377011 |
| Macao SAR, China | 3.361538458 |
| Madagascar | 2.387265703 |
| Malawi | 3.020189257 |
| Malaysia | 6.993458832 |
| Maldives | *not enough data* |
| Mali | 3.985437368 |
| Malta | 5.076343387 |
| Mauritania | 2.549565422 |
| Mauritius | 5.20483739 |
| Mexico | 3.465007677 |
| Moldova | -6.251362832 |
| Mongolia | 0.38666376 |
| Montenegro | *not enough data* |
| Morocco | 3.348326072 |
| Mozambique | 7.392397747 |
| Myanmar | 6.921814059 |
| Namibia | 3.234835794 |
| Nepal | 4.906089847 |
| Netherlands | 3.376149948 |
| New Zealand | 2.641633436 |
| Nicaragua | 2.721804863 |
| Niger | 1.955267849 |
| Nigeria | 3.265903504 |
| Norway | 3.225039703 |
| Oman | 4.808520207 |
| Pakistan | 3.919808467 |
| Panama | 4.704571173 |
| Papua New Guinea | 3.007368954 |
| Paraguay | 2.668900972 |

| | |
|---|---|
| Peru | 1.772207721 |
| Philippines | *not enough data* |
| Poland | *not enough data* |
| Portugal | 3.183605039 |
| Qatar | *not enough data* |
| Romania | *not enough data* |
| Russian Federation | *not enough data* |
| Rwanda | 2.908670222 |
| Sao Tome and Principe | *not enough data* |
| Saudi Arabia | 2.806968676 |
| Senegal | 2.993064976 |
| Seychelles | 4.545094885 |
| Sierra Leone | -1.996820231 |
| Singapore | 7.010095099 |
| Slovak Republic | *not enough data* |
| Slovenia | *not enough data* |
| Solomon Islands | *not enough data* |
| South Africa | 1.781180022 |
| Spain | 3.126010187 |
| Sri Lanka | 4.566023751 |
| St. Kitts and Nevis | 4.325982174 |
| St. Lucia | 5.02420705 |
| St. Martin (French part) | *not enough data* |
| St. Vincent and the Grenadines | 2.982979936 |
| Suriname | 1.722153991 |
| Swaziland | 4.97430539 |
| Sweden | 2.048091705 |
| Switzerland | 1.658807186 |
| Chinese Taipei | *data unavailable* |
| Tajikistan | -6.215384727 |
| Tanzania | 3.643031864 |
| Thailand | 5.54652273 |
| Togo | 2.142562201 |
| Tonga | 2.374305096 |
| Trinidad and Tobago | 3.875578525 |
| Tunisia | 4.696782165 |
| Turkey | 3.165451222 |
| Uganda | 6.424508048 |

| | |
|---|---|
| Ukraine | -5.380148215 |
| United Arab Emirates | 6.08853304 |
| United Kingdom | 2.5129679 |
| United States | 3.159219881 |
| Uruguay | 2.484168802 |
| Vanuatu | 3.392430272 |
| Venezuela, RB | 1.780294958 |
| Vietnam | 7.271912916 |
| Yemen, Rep. | *not enough data* |
| Zambia | 1.639158487 |
| Zimbabwe | 2.510640155 |
| European Union | 2.461259566 |
| | **3.101241111** |

The countries that had the best annual GDP mean performance from 1989 to 2001 are

shown below.

| Country Name | GDP Mean 1989-2001 |
|---|---|
| Cabo Verde | 9.504301006 |
| China | 9.311780299 |
| Mozambique | 7.392397747 |
| Vietnam | 7.271912916 |
| Ireland | 7.216977262 |
| Singapore | 7.010095099 |
| Malaysia | 6.993458832 |
| Myanmar | 6.921814059 |
| Belize | 6.836949903 |
| Lao PDR | 6.806081578 |

The countries that had the worst annual GDP mean performance from 1989 to 2001 are

shown below.

| Country Name | GDP Mean 1989-2001 |
|---|---|
| Georgia | -6.980494665 |
| Moldova | -6.251362832 |
| Tajikistan | -6.215384727 |
| Ukraine | -5.380148215 |

| Country Name | GDP Mean 2002-2014 |
|---|---|
| Congo, Dem. Rep. | -4.997698797 |
| Russian Federation | -2.830654114 |
| Sierra Leone | -1.996820231 |
| Kyrgyz Republic | -1.591536826 |
| Burundi | -0.906530597 |
| Cuba | -0.782850534 |

The annual GDP mean performance for all countries who were world trade organization members by 2016 was calculated individually from 2002 to 2014 and, then, averaged. An average for all member nations was also calculated to derive a base mean for WTO's members performance for this period, and member nations that failed to report annual GDP data for each established time frame analyzed were not included in this research. All nations included in this analysis reported national annual GDP data to the World Bank in 12 out of the 12 years studied. The average GDP mean for all member nations from the years 2002 to 2014 was 3.98.

| Country Name | GDP Mean 2002-2014 |
|---|---|
| Albania | 4.200480835 |
| Angola | *not enough data* |
| Antigua and Barbuda | 2.359754509 |
| Argentina | 4.434059798 |
| Armenia | 7.08906658 |
| Australia | 3.04005939 |
| Austria | 1.395975154 |
| Bahrain | 5.142389819 |
| Bangladesh | 5.828453736 |
| Barbados | 1.048899107 |
| Belgium | 1.434693085 |
| Belize | 3.512692585 |
| Benin | 4.193767524 |
| Bolivia | 4.566784375 |
| Botswana | 5.106034757 |
| Brazil | 3.433064673 |

| | |
|---|---|
| Brunei Darussalam | 0.877008274 |
| Bulgaria | 3.495996432 |
| Burkina Faso | 5.886659662 |
| Burundi | 3.761180688 |
| Cabo Verde | 5.033380159 |
| Cambodia | 7.799371353 |
| Cameroon | 3.755457047 |
| Canada | 2.063321989 |
| Central African Republic | -0.572636895 |
| Chad | 9.298498454 |
| Chile | 4.055133657 |
| China | 9.930601164 |
| Colombia | 4.565567226 |
| Congo, Dem. Rep. | 6.208615572 |
| Congo, Rep. | 4.655027718 |
| Costa Rica | 4.57405269 |
| Cote d'Ivoire | 2.700226996 |
| Croatia | 1.389341888 |
| Cuba | not enough data |
| Cyprus | 1.29963754 |
| Czech Republic | 2.440374652 |
| Denmark | 0.574761357 |
| Djibouti | 4.411079064 |
| Dominica | 2.165657905 |
| Dominican Republic | 5.015845612 |
| Ecuador | 4.546396546 |
| Egypt, Arab Rep. | 4.106219635 |
| El Salvador | 1.939147044 |
| Estonia | 3.595392752 |
| Fiji | 1.898764843 |
| Finland | 1.12946317 |
| France | 1.029704438 |
| Gabon | 2.81893769 |
| Gambia, The | 3.106488387 |
| Georgia | 6.151998314 |
| Germany | 1.048742318 |
| Ghana | 6.806071989 |
| Greece | -0.368343853 |
| Grenada | 2.240793191 |
| Guatemala | 3.557639732 |

| | |
|---|---|
| Guinea | 2.550064665 |
| Guinea-Bissau | 2.518479482 |
| Guyana | not enough data |
| Haiti | *1.370275065* |
| Honduras | 4.05477804 |
| Hong Kong SAR, China | 4.06333125 |
| Hungary | 1.731024652 |
| Iceland | 2.552136508 |
| India | 7.421030206 |
| Indonesia | 5.501492594 |
| Ireland | 2.641640315 |
| Israel | 3.546962581 |
| Italy | -0.217399168 |
| Jamaica | 0.610085685 |
| Japan | 0.801266029 |
| Jordan | 5.318082928 |
| Kazakhstan | 7.130769231 |
| Kenya | 4.72591074 |
| Korea, Rep. | 4.003284039 |
| Kuwait | 4.883735767 |
| Kyrgyz Republic | 4.362538586 |
| Lao PDR | 7.505378426 |
| Latvia | 3.870219485 |
| Lesotho | 4.106580651 |
| Liechtenstein | *not enough data* |
| Lithuania | *4.306282144* |
| Luxembourg | 2.749488361 |
| Macao SAR, China | 12.2342128 |
| Madagascar | 2.436397205 |
| Malawi | 5.191249487 |
| Malaysia | 5.1843119 |
| Maldives | 7.090048773 |
| Mali | 4.367571967 |
| Malta | 1.950765629 |
| Mauritania | 5.40827235 |
| Mauritius | 3.78015728 |
| Mexico | 2.343983753 |
| Moldova | 5.057245246 |
| Mongolia | 8.576687919 |
| Montenegro | 3.214146029 |

| | |
|---|---|
| Morocco | 4.404602601 |
| Mozambique | 7.515159205 |
| Myanmar | *not enough data* |
| Namibia | *5.285416702* |
| Nepal | 4.013067579 |
| Netherlands | 0.942477985 |
| New Zealand | 2.454916352 |
| Nicaragua | 3.551506321 |
| Niger | 4.976720612 |
| Nigeria | 8.328758113 |
| Norway | 1.561398087 |
| Oman | 3.211493986 |
| Pakistan | 4.278290935 |
| Panama | 7.40712873 |
| Papua New Guinea | 5.674796951 |
| Paraguay | 4.466728524 |
| Peru | 5.851971998 |
| Philippines | 5.26274734 |
| Poland | 3.7311988 |
| Portugal | -0.038584171 |
| Qatar | 12.13820867 |
| Romania | 3.596786253 |
| Russian Federation | 4.143228731 |
| Rwanda | 7.592289805 |
| Sao Tome and Principe | 5.154614654 |
| Saudi Arabia | 5.5797297 |
| Senegal | 3.921816934 |
| Seychelles | 3.682721307 |
| Sierra Leone | 9.175773867 |
| Singapore | 5.928084078 |
| Slovak Republic | 4.190457732 |
| Slovenia | 1.868699401 |
| Solomon Islands | 4.589176484 |
| South Africa | 3.177893418 |
| Spain | 1.117273419 |
| Sri Lanka | 6.074210713 |
| St. Kitts and Nevis | 2.335321549 |
| St. Lucia | 1.689560422 |
| St. Martin (French part) | *not enough data* |
| St. Vincent and the | 2.399540815 |

| | |
|---|---|
| Grenadines | |
| Suriname | 4.494141226 |
| Swaziland | 2.404029962 |
| Sweden | 1.991507546 |
| Switzerland | 1.839724552 |
| Chinese Taipei | *data unavailable* |
| Tajikistan | 7.753788504 |
| Tanzania | 6.750608354 |
| Thailand | 4.19569941 |
| Togo | 3.46375423 |
| Tonga | 0.924841511 |
| Trinidad and Tobago | 4.410427926 |
| Tunisia | 3.558410736 |
| Turkey | 4.904028897 |
| Uganda | 6.98796523 |
| Ukraine | 2.684614815 |
| United Arab Emirates | 4.558053334 |
| United Kingdom | 1.66894009 |
| United States | 1.858759643 |
| Uruguay | 4.037286915 |
| Vanuatu | 3.134639431 |
| Venezuela, RB | 2.950117993 |
| Vietnam | 6.36823974 |
| Yemen, Rep. | *not enough data* |
| Zambia | 7.311541048 |
| Zimbabwe | -1.079090737 |
| European Union | 1.144316488 |
| | **3.988777743** |

The countries that had the best annual GDP mean performance from 2002 to 2014 are shown below.

| Country Name | GDP Mean 2002-2014 |
|---|---|
| Macao SAR, China | 12.2342128 |
| Qatar | 12.13820867 |
| China | 9.930601164 |
| Chad | 9.298498454 |

| | |
|---|---|
| Sierra Leone | 9.175773867 |
| Mongolia | 8.576687919 |
| Nigeria | 8.328758113 |
| Cambodia | 7.799371353 |
| Tajikistan | 7.753788504 |
| Rwanda | 7.592289805 |
| | **9.282819065** |

The countries that had the worst GDP performance from 2002 to 2014 are shown below.

| Country Name | GDP Mean 2002-2014 |
|---|---|
| Greece | -1.239518088 |
| Central African Republic | -0.519661276 |
| Italy | -0.287251327 |
| Portugal | -0.031230692 |
| Jamaica | 0.239799255 |
| Brunei Darussalam | 0.458505288 |
| Denmark | 0.599189118 |
| Tonga | 0.614594398 |
| Croatia | 0.720533739 |
| Japan | 0.770255353 |
| | **0.132521577** |

The data from the countries with the best GDP performance from 1989 to 2001 was then compared to their GDP performance from 2002 to 2014 as well as the statistical mean for each data set.

| Country Name | GDP Mean 1989-2001 | GDP Mean 2002-2014 |
|---|---|---|
| Cabo Verde | 9.504301006 | 5.033380159 |
| China | 9.311780299 | 9.930601164 |
| Mozambique | 7.392397747 | 7.515159205 |
| Vietnam | 7.271912916 | 6.36823974 |

| | | |
|---|---|---|
| Ireland | 7.216977262 | 2.641640315 |
| Singapore | 7.010095099 | 5.928084078 |
| Malaysia | 6.993458832 | 5.1843119 |
| Myanmar | 6.921814059 | *not enough data* |
| Belize | 6.836949903 | 3.512692585 |
| Lao PDR | 6.806081578 | 7.505378426 |
| | **7.52657687** | **5.957720841** |

The data from the 10 countries with the worst GDP performance from 1989 to 2001 was then compared to their GDP performance from 2002 to 2014 as well as the statistical mean for each data set.

| Country Name | GDP Mean 1989-2001 | GDP Mean 2002-2014 |
|---|---|---|
| Georgia | -6.980494665 | 6.151998314 |
| Moldova | -6.251362832 | 5.057245246 |
| Tajikistan | -6.215384727 | 7.753788504 |
| Ukraine | -5.380148215 | 2.684614815 |
| Congo, Dem. Rep. | -4.997698797 | 6.208615572 |
| Russian Federation | -2.830654114 | 4.143228731 |
| Sierra Leone | -1.996820231 | 9.175773867 |
| Kyrgyz Republic | -1.591536826 | 4.362538586 |
| Burundi | -0.906530597 | 3.761180688 |
| Cuba | -0.782850534 | 4.831512942 |
| | **-3.793348154** | **5.413049727** |

The data from the countries that had the best GDP performance from 2002 to 2014 was then compared to their GDP performance from 1989 to 2001 as well as the statistical mean for each data set.

| Country Name | GDP Mean 1989-2001 | GDP Mean 2002-2014 |
|---|---|---|
| Macao SAR, China | 3.36 | 12.23 |
| Qatar | *not enough data* | 12.14 |

| | | |
|---|---|---|
| China | 9.31 | 9.93 |
| Chad | 2.91 | 9.30 |
| Sierra Leone | -2.00 | 9.18 |
| Mongolia | 0.39 | 8.58 |
| Nigeria | 3.27 | 8.33 |
| Cambodia | *not enough data* | 7.80 |
| Tajikistan | -6.22 | 7.75 |
| Rwanda | 2.91 | 7.59 |
| | **1.741462101** | **9.282819065** |

The data from the countries that had the worst GDP performance from 2002 to 2014 was then compared to their GDP performance from 1989 to 2001 as well as the statistical mean for each data set.

| Country Name | GDP Mean 1989-2001 | GDP Mean 2002-2014 |
|---|---|---|
| Greece | 2.497079815 | -1.239518088 |
| Central African Republic | 1.297202206 | -0.519661276 |
| Italy | 1.824300893 | -0.287251327 |
| Portugal | 3.183605039 | -0.031230692 |
| Jamaica | 2.384664038 | 0.239799255 |
| Brunei Darussalam | 1.949438381 | 0.458505288 |
| Denmark | 2.296494483 | 0.599189118 |
| Tonga | 2.374305096 | 0.614594398 |
| Croatia | *not enough data* | 0.720533739 |
| Japan | 1.744543148 | 0.770255353 |
| | **2.172403678** | **0.132521577** |

The percentage of change for the annual GDP mean performance for all countries who were world trade organization members by 2016 was then calculated individually from the time period of 1989 to 2001 against the time period of 2002 to 2014.

| Country Name | GDP Mean 1989-2001 | GDP Mean 2002-2014 | % of Change |
|---|---|---|---|
| Albania | 2.311617942 | 4.200480835 | 0.817117249 |

| | | | |
|---|---|---|---|
| Angola | 1.352123317 | *not enough data* | *not enough data* |
| Antigua and Barbuda | 3.134286381 | 2.359754509 | -0.247115859 |
| Argentina | 2.501374337 | 4.434059798 | 0.772649432 |
| Armenia | *not enough data* | 7.08906658 | *not enough data* |
| Australia | 3.272611315 | 3.04005939 | -0.07106005 |
| Austria | 2.756691749 | 1.395975154 | -0.493604914 |
| Bahrain | 4.873541092 | 5.142389819 | 0.055164966 |
| Bangladesh | 4.641561628 | 5.828453736 | 0.255709652 |
| Barbados | 0.798559926 | 1.048899107 | 0.313488284 |
| Belgium | 2.300586939 | 1.434693085 | -0.37637954 |
| Belize | 6.836949903 | 3.512692585 | -0.486219347 |
| Benin | 4.44300709 | 4.193767524 | -0.056097044 |
| Bolivia | 3.685936611 | 4.566784375 | 0.238975288 |
| Botswana | 5.328176416 | 5.106034757 | -0.041691874 |
| Brazil | 2.139919138 | 3.433064673 | 0.604296448 |
| Brunei Darussalam | 1.949438381 | 0.877008274 | -0.550122598 |
| Bulgaria | -1.329080131 | 3.495996432 | -3.630388003 |
| Burkina Faso | 4.755378365 | 5.886659662 | 0.237895118 |
| Burundi | -0.906530597 | 3.761180688 | -5.148983719 |
| Cabo Verde | 9.504301006 | 5.033380159 | -0.470410275 |
| Cambodia | *not enough data* | 7.799371353 | *not enough data* |
| Cameroon | 0.869067276 | 3.755457047 | 3.321250093 |
| Canada | 2.539873857 | 2.063321989 | -0.187628164 |
| Central African Republic | 1.297202206 | -0.572636895 | -1.441439964 |
| Chad | 2.909345526 | 9.298498454 | 2.196079108 |
| Chile | 6.320067352 | 4.055133657 | -0.358371765 |
| China | 9.311780299 | 9.930601164 | 0.066455699 |
| Colombia | 2.932544795 | 4.565567226 | 0.556861888 |
| Congo, Dem. Rep. | -4.997698797 | 6.208615572 | -2.242294869 |
| Congo, Rep. | 1.716874318 | 4.655027718 | 1.711338663 |
| Costa Rica | 4.824672024 | 4.57405269 | -0.051945362 |
| Cote d'Ivoire | 1.958998992 | 2.700226996 | 0.378370794 |
| Croatia | *not enough data* | 1.389341888 | *not enough data* |
| Cuba | -0.782850534 | *not enough data* | *not enough data* |
| Cyprus | 4.711197845 | 1.29963754 | -0.72413862 |
| Czech Republic | *not enough data* | 2.440374652 | *not enough data* |
| Denmark | 2.296494483 | 0.574761357 | -0.7497223 |
| Djibouti | *not enough data* | 4.411079064 | *not enough data* |
| Dominica | 1.799723482 | 2.165657905 | 0.203328137 |
| Dominican Republic | 4.750037102 | 5.015845612 | 0.055959249 |
| Ecuador | 2.251503827 | 4.546396546 | 1.019271072 |
| Egypt, Arab Rep. | 4.402023761 | 4.106219635 | -0.067197303 |

| | | | |
|---|---|---|---|
| El Salvador | 4.133946872 | 1.939147044 | -0.53092115 |
| Estonia | *not enough data* | 3.595392752 | *not enough data* |
| Fiji | 3.028358746 | 1.898764843 | -0.373005313 |
| Finland | 2.456558114 | 1.12946317 | -0.540225341 |
| France | 2.32631411 | 1.029704438 | -0.557366551 |
| Gabon | 2.58107361 | 2.81893769 | 0.092157031 |
| Gambia, The | 3.716320604 | 3.106488387 | -0.164095696 |
| Georgia | -6.980494665 | 6.151998314 | -1.881312659 |
| Germany | 2.362603226 | 1.048742318 | -0.556107303 |
| Ghana | 4.264427823 | 6.806071989 | 0.596010595 |
| Greece | 2.497079815 | -0.368343853 | -1.147509844 |
| Grenada | 3.155316376 | 2.240793191 | -0.289835654 |
| Guatemala | 3.888851239 | 3.557639732 | -0.085169498 |
| Guinea | 3.930348983 | 2.550064665 | -0.351186198 |
| Guinea-Bissau | 2.057034761 | 2.518479482 | 0.224325194 |
| Guyana | 3.369386179 | not enough data | *not enough data* |
| Haiti | *not enough data* | *1.370275065* | *not enough data* |
| Honduras | 3.104705697 | 4.05477804 | 0.306010436 |
| Hong Kong SAR, China | 3.604751076 | 4.06333125 | 0.12721549 |
| Hungary | *not enough data* | 1.731024652 | *not enough data* |
| Iceland | 2.44131016 | 2.552136508 | 0.045396259 |
| India | 5.561437644 | 7.421030206 | 0.334372635 |
| Indonesia | 5.076590863 | 5.501492594 | 0.083698242 |
| Ireland | 7.216977262 | 2.641640315 | -0.633968597 |
| Israel | 5.194818351 | 3.546962581 | -0.317211432 |
| Italy | 1.824300893 | -0.217399168 | -1.119168482 |
| Jamaica | 2.384664038 | 0.610085685 | -0.744162836 |
| Japan | 1.744543148 | 0.801266029 | -0.540701513 |
| Jordan | 3.469609584 | 5.318082928 | 0.532761194 |
| Kazakhstan | *not enough data* | 7.130769231 | *not enough data* |
| Kenya | 2.423876636 | 4.72591074 | 0.949732371 |
| Korea, Rep. | 6.683490592 | 4.003284039 | -0.401018976 |
| Kuwait | *not enough data* | 4.883735767 | *not enough data* |
| Kyrgyz Republic | -1.591536826 | 4.362538586 | -3.741085544 |
| Lao PDR | 6.806081578 | 7.505378426 | 0.102745881 |
| Latvia | *not enough data* | 3.870219485 | *not enough data* |
| Lesotho | 4.13611013 | 4.106580651 | -0.007139432 |
| Liechtenstein | 4.924449166 | *not enough data* | *not enough data* |
| Lithuania | *not enough data* | *4.306282144* | *not enough data* |
| Luxembourg | 5.230377011 | 2.749488361 | -0.474323102 |
| Macao SAR, China | 3.361538458 | 12.2342128 | 2.639468343 |
| Madagascar | 2.387265703 | 2.436397205 | 0.020580659 |

| | | | |
|---|---|---|---|
| Malawi | 3.020189257 | 5.191249487 | 0.718849067 |
| Malaysia | 6.993458832 | 5.1843119 | -0.258691296 |
| Maldives | *not enough data* | 7.090048773 | *not enough data* |
| Mali | 3.985437368 | 4.367571967 | 0.095882726 |
| Malta | 5.076343387 | 1.950765629 | -0.615714407 |
| Mauritania | 2.549565422 | 5.40827235 | 1.121252627 |
| Mauritius | 5.20483739 | 3.78015728 | -0.273722309 |
| Mexico | 3.465007677 | 2.343983753 | -0.323527111 |
| Moldova | -6.251362832 | 5.057245246 | -1.808982838 |
| Mongolia | 0.38666376 | 8.576687919 | 21.18125619 |
| Montenegro | *not enough data* | 3.214146029 | *not enough data* |
| Morocco | 3.348326072 | 4.404602601 | 0.315464058 |
| Mozambique | 7.392397747 | 7.515159205 | 0.016606447 |
| Myanmar | 6.921814059 | *not enough data* | *not enough data* |
| Namibia | 3.234835794 | *5.285416702* | 0.633905718 |
| Nepal | 4.906089847 | 4.013067579 | -0.182023219 |
| Netherlands | 3.376149948 | 0.942477985 | -0.72084238 |
| New Zealand | 2.641633436 | 2.454916352 | -0.070682435 |
| Nicaragua | 2.721804863 | 3.551506321 | 0.304835027 |
| Niger | 1.955267849 | 4.976720612 | 1.545288419 |
| Nigeria | 3.265903504 | 8.328758113 | 1.550215615 |
| Norway | 3.225039703 | 1.561398087 | -0.515851515 |
| Oman | 4.808520207 | 3.211493986 | -0.332124261 |
| Pakistan | 3.919808467 | 4.278290935 | 0.091454078 |
| Panama | 4.704571173 | 7.40712873 | 0.574453538 |
| Papua New Guinea | 3.007368954 | 5.674796951 | 0.886964 |
| Paraguay | 2.668900972 | 4.466728524 | 0.673620929 |
| Peru | 1.772207721 | 5.851971998 | 2.302080184 |
| Philippines | *not enough data* | 5.26274734 | *not enough data* |
| Poland | *not enough data* | 3.7311988 | *not enough data* |
| Portugal | 3.183605039 | -0.038584171 | -1.012119648 |
| Qatar | *not enough data* | 12.13820867 | *not enough data* |
| Romania | *not enough data* | 3.596786253 | *not enough data* |
| Russian Federation | *not enough data* | 4.143228731 | *not enough data* |
| Rwanda | 2.908670222 | 7.592289805 | 1.610227089 |
| Sao Tome and Principe | *not enough data* | 5.154614654 | *not enough data* |
| Saudi Arabia | 2.806968676 | 5.5797297 | 0.987813312 |
| Senegal | 2.993064976 | 3.921816934 | 0.310301302 |
| Seychelles | 4.545094885 | 3.682721307 | -0.1897372 |
| Sierra Leone | -1.996820231 | 9.175773867 | -5.595192759 |
| Singapore | 7.010095099 | 5.928084078 | -0.154350405 |
| Slovak Republic | *not enough data* | 4.190457732 | *not enough data* |

| | | |
|---|---|---|
| Slovenia | *not enough data* | 1.868699401 | *not enough data* |
| Solomon Islands | *not enough data* | 4.589176484 | *not enough data* |
| South Africa | 1.781180022 | 3.177893418 | 0.784150607 |
| Spain | 3.126010187 | 1.117273419 | -0.642588043 |
| Sri Lanka | 4.566023751 | 6.074210713 | 0.330306421 |
| St. Kitts and Nevis | 4.325982174 | 2.335321549 | -0.460163853 |
| St. Lucia | 5.02420705 | 1.689560422 | -0.663716004 |
| St. Martin (French part) | *not enough data* | *not enough data* | *not enough data* |
| St. Vincent and the Grenadines | 2.982979936 | 2.399540815 | -0.195589355 |
| Suriname | 1.722153991 | 4.494141226 | 1.609604745 |
| Swaziland | 4.97430539 | 2.404029962 | -0.51671042 |
| Sweden | 2.048091705 | 1.991507546 | -0.027627747 |
| Switzerland | 1.658807186 | 1.839724552 | 0.109064735 |
| Chinese Taipei | *data unavailable* | *data unavailable* | *data unavailable* |
| Tajikistan | -6.215384727 | 7.753788504 | -2.247515455 |
| Tanzania | 3.643031864 | 6.750608354 | 0.8530193 |
| Thailand | 5.54652273 | 4.19569941 | -0.243544178 |
| Togo | 2.142562201 | 3.46375423 | 0.616641154 |
| Tonga | 2.374305096 | 0.924841511 | -0.610479078 |
| Trinidad and Tobago | 3.875578525 | 4.410427926 | 0.138005048 |
| Tunisia | 4.696782165 | 3.558410736 | -0.242372626 |
| Turkey | 3.165451222 | 4.904028897 | 0.549235339 |
| Uganda | 6.424508048 | 6.98796523 | 0.087704331 |
| Ukraine | -5.380148215 | 2.684614815 | -1.49898529 |
| United Arab Emirates | 6.08853304 | 4.558053334 | -0.251370847 |
| United Kingdom | 2.5129679 | 1.66894009 | -0.335868918 |
| United States | 3.159219881 | 1.858759643 | -0.411639673 |
| Uruguay | 2.484168802 | 4.037286915 | 0.625206351 |
| Vanuatu | 3.392430272 | 3.134639431 | -0.075990019 |
| Venezuela, RB | 1.780294958 | 2.950117993 | 0.657095067 |
| Vietnam | 7.271912916 | 6.36823974 | -0.124268977 |
| Yemen, Rep. | *not enough data* | *not enough data* | *not enough data* |
| Zambia | 1.639158487 | 7.311541048 | 3.460545521 |
| Zimbabwe | 2.510640155 | -1.079090737 | -1.42980701 |
| European Union | 2.461259566 | 1.144316488 | -0.535068749 |
| | **3.101241111** | **3.988777743** | **0.286187562** |

The percentage of change of the annual GDP mean performance for the 10 countries with the best GDP performance from 1989 to 2001 was measured against their performance from 2002 to 2014.

| Country Name | GDP Mean 1989-2001 | GDP Mean 2002-2014 | % of Change |
|---|---|---|---|
| Cabo Verde | 9.504301006 | 5.033380159 | -0.470410275 |
| China | 9.311780299 | 9.930601164 | 0.066455699 |
| Mozambique | 7.392397747 | 7.515159205 | 0.016606447 |
| Vietnam | 7.271912916 | 6.36823974 | -0.124268977 |
| Ireland | 7.216977262 | 2.641640315 | -0.633968597 |
| Singapore | 7.010095099 | 5.928084078 | -0.154350405 |
| Malaysia | 6.993458832 | 5.1843119 | -0.258691296 |
| Myanmar | 6.921814059 | *not enough data* | *not enough data* |
| Belize | 6.836949903 | 3.512692585 | -0.486219347 |
| Lao PDR | 6.806081578 | 7.505378426 | 0.102745881 |
| | **7.52657687** | **5.957720841** | **-0.208442172** |

The percentage of change of the annual GDP mean performance for the 10 countries with the worst GDP performance from 1989 to 2001 was measured against their performance from 2002 to 2014.

| Country Name | GDP Mean 1989-2001 | GDP Mean 2002-2014 | % of Change |
|---|---|---|---|
| Georgia | -6.980494665 | 6.151998314 | -1.881312659 |
| Moldova | -6.251362832 | 5.057245246 | -1.808982838 |
| Tajikistan | -6.215384727 | 7.753788504 | -2.247515455 |
| Ukraine | -5.380148215 | 2.684614815 | -1.49898529 |
| Congo, Dem. Rep. | -4.997698797 | 6.208615572 | -2.242294869 |
| Russian Federation | -2.830654114 | 4.143228731 | -2.463700108 |
| Sierra Leone | -1.996820231 | 9.175773867 | -5.595192759 |
| Kyrgyz Republic | -1.591536826 | 4.362538586 | -3.741085544 |
| Burundi | -0.906530597 | 3.761180688 | -5.148983719 |
| Cuba | -0.782850534 | 4.831512942 | -7.171692721 |
| | **-3.793348154** | **5.413049727** | **-2.426984687** |

The percentage of change of the annual GDP mean performance for the 10 countries with the best GDP performance from 2002 to 2014 was measured against their performance from 1989 to 2001.

| Country Name | GDP Mean 1989-2001 | GDP Mean 2002-2014 | % of Change |
|---|---|---|---|
| Macao SAR, China | 3.361538458 | 12.2342128 | 2.639468343 |
| Qatar | *not enough data* | 12.13820867 | *not enough data* |
| China | 9.311780299 | 9.930601164 | 0.066455699 |
| Chad | 2.909345526 | 9.298498454 | 2.196079108 |
| Sierra Leone | -1.996820231 | 9.175773867 | -5.595192759 |
| Mongolia | 0.38666376 | 8.576687919 | 21.1812562 |
| Nigeria | 3.265903504 | 8.328758113 | 1.550215614 |
| Cambodia | *not enough data* | 7.799371353 | *not enough data* |
| Tajikistan | -6.215384727 | 7.753788504 | -2.247515455 |
| Rwanda | 2.908670222 | 7.592289805 | 1.610227089 |
| **1.741462101** | **9.282819065** | **4.330474351** |

The percentage of change of the annual GDP mean performance for the 10 countries with the worst GDP performance from 2002 to 2014 was measured against their performance from 1989 to 2001.

| Country Name | GDP Mean 1989-2001 | GDP Mean 2002-2014 | % of Change |
|---|---|---|---|
| Greece | 2.497079815 | -1.239518088 | -1.496387052 |
| Central African Republic | 1.297202206 | -0.519661276 | -1.400601597 |
| Italy | 1.824300893 | -0.287251327 | -1.157458305 |
| Portugal | 3.183605039 | -0.031230692 | -1.009809851 |
| Jamaica | 2.384664038 | 0.239799255 | -0.899441074 |
| Brunei Darussalam | 1.949438381 | 0.458505288 | -0.764801344 |
| Denmark | 2.296494483 | 0.599189118 | -0.739085322 |
| Tonga | 2.374305096 | 0.614594398 | -0.741147673 |
| Croatia | *not enough data* | 0.720533739 | *not enough data* |
| Japan | 1.744543148 | 0.770255353 | -0.558477327 |

**2.172403678**     **0.132521577**     **-0.93899772**

The top 10 countries with the largest positive annual GDP mean performance gain between 1989 to 2001 and 2002 to 2014 was calculated.

| Country Name | Positive GDP of Gains Between 1989-2001 and 2002-2014 |
|---|---|
| Tajikistan | 13.97 |
| Georgia | 13.13 |
| Moldova | 11.31 |
| Congo, Dem. Rep. | 11.21 |
| Sierra Leone | 11.17 |
| Macao SAR, China | 8.87 |
| Mongolia | 8.19 |
| Ukraine | 8.06 |
| Chad | 6.39 |
| Kyrgyz Republic | 5.95 |

The top 10 countries with the largest negative annual GDP mean performance loss between 1989 to 2001 and 2002 to 2014 was calculated.

| Country Name | Negative GDP of Losses Between 1989-2001 and 2002-2014 |
|---|---|
| Ireland | -4.58 |
| Cabo Verde | -4.47 |
| Zimbabwe | -3.59 |
| Cyprus | -3.41 |
| St. Lucia | -3.33 |
| Belize | -3.32 |
| Portugal | -3.22 |
| Malta | -3.13 |
| Greece | -2.87 |
| Korea, Rep. | -2.68 |

## Discussion

The annual GDP mean performance between all member nations from 1989 to 2001 was compared to the annual GDP mean performance between all member nations from 2002 to 2012. The GDP mean for all member nations rose by .29 when comparing the two time periods, 1989 to 2001 and 2002 to 2012.

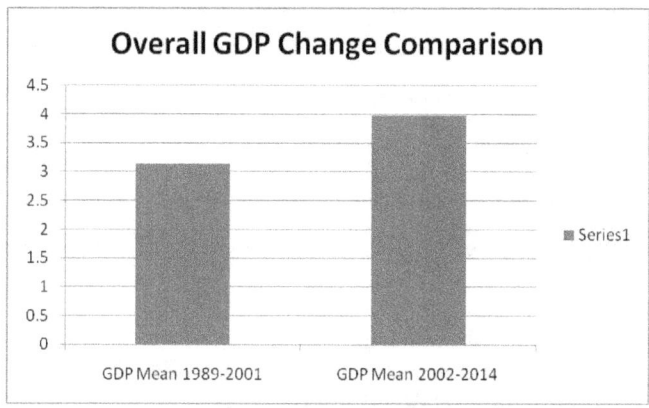

As can be seen in the chart above, the annual GDP mean performance of all member countries for the two given periods difference is 0.29, which means the average annual GDP mean performance increase of all member countries from the first data set to the second data set was 29%. This is a substantial increase, and it is clear there were a number of factors that contributed to this growth. It is clear that the WTO has made the world a more prosperous place, and it has assisted governments in resisting national pressure to return to protectionists policies embraced prior to the formation of the organization (Porter, 2015). The WTO has resulted in strengthening developing economies and weakening developed ones in many ways, but it is clear from the data in this study that it has made the world economy and free trade grow as can be seen in the percentage of growth between the two time periods above. The result of bilateral, regional, and unilateral trade agreements has weakened the WTO organization, and, in many ways, it sits on the sidelines in today's global economy. This has resulted from many factors, but it is due to frustration over the current policies and national pressure to maintain strong annual GDP growth within nations. The nations with the best annual GDP mean performance from 1989 to 2001 were then extracted from the 162 nations measured, and there performance was then compared to their annual GDP mean performance from 2002 to 2014.

A comparison 10 countries with the best annual GDP mean performance from 1989 to 2001 was compared to their annual GDP mean performance from 2002 to 2014.

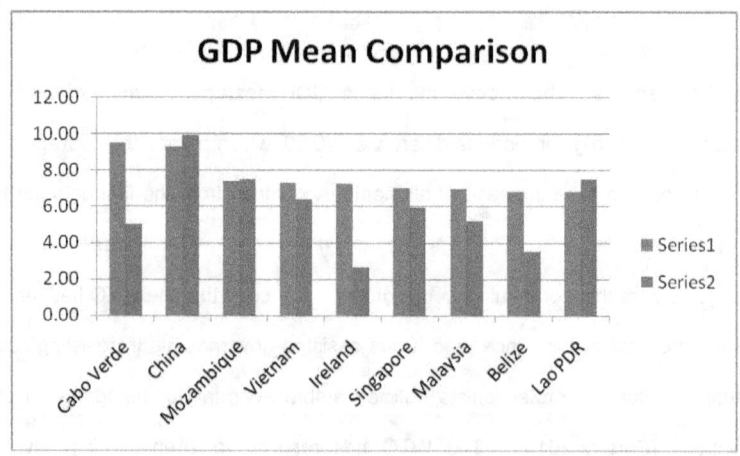

In the above chart, Series 1 represents the annual GDP mean performance from 1989 to 2001 of the top performing countries from this time period, and Series 2 represents the annual GDP mean performance of the same nations from 2002 to 2014. Myanmar was not included in this analysis because it failed to report all of its annual GDP performance data to the World Bank from 2002 to 2014. There is clearly a dramatic shift with an average decline of the entire group's annual GDP mean performance between the two time periods has declined 21%. The most important changes of annual GDP mean performance from the two time periods of note in the chart shown above are Ireland, Cabo Verde, and Belize. Ireland joined the WTO in 1995 and became a GATT member in 1967, and it is clear that their economy has suffered dramatically between the two periods analyzed. Ireland's annual GDP mean performance shifted 63% between the two periods, which represents a decrease in annual GDP mean performance by 4.58. This suggests that membership in the WTO may no longer be benefitting the nation as it has in the past, and that they have not established significant bilateral, regional, and unilateral trade agreements necessary to maintain economic competitiveness in the twenty-first century despite their membership in the WTO. Cabo Verde joined the WTO organization in 2008, and Cabo Verde's annual GDP mean performance shifted 47% between the two periods, which represents a decrease in annual GDP mean performance by 4.47. The decline in Cabo Verde's annual GDP mean performance over the two periods suggests that in fact joining the WTO has not helped the nation's economic growth. Belize joined the WTO in 1995, and it became a GATT member in 1983. Belize's annual GDP mean performance shifted 49% between the two periods, which represents a decrease in annual GDP mean performance by 3.32. Its economy is clearly suffering from similar economic woes that Ireland has faced, and the data suggests that, despite being a member of the WTO, they have not developed the necessary bilateral, regional, and unilateral trade agreements to maintain economic strength in the twenty-first century. Also, the data suggests that there may be little benefit to the nation in maintaining WTO membership in the future in relation to its annual GDP mean performance. The nations with the worst performing annual GDP mean performance from 1989 to 2001 were then extracted from the 162 nations measured, and there performance was then compared to their annual GDP mean performance from 2002 to 2014.

A comparison 10 countries with the worst annual GDP mean performance from 1989 to 2001 was compared to their annual GDP performance from 2002 to 2014.

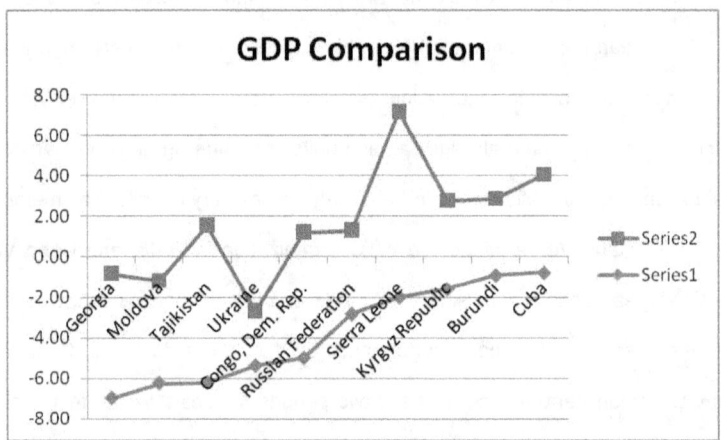

The nations with the worst annual GDP mean performance from 1989 to 2001 is compared to their annual GDP mean performance from 2002 to 2014. Important annual GDP mean performance shift were seen from Tajikistan, Georgia, and Moldova. The group's annual GDP mean performance positively shifted 243% overall from 1989 to

2001 in comparison to 2002 to 2014. This is a remarkable gain, and it shows that membership in the WTO has benefitted nations that were once suffering. All members of this group show large shifts in their annual GDP mean performance from 1989 to 2001 in comparison to 2002 to 2014. Tajikistan who joined the WTO in 2013 has shown the largest reversal in GDP performance, but it is not clear if this is a result of membership in the WTO or bilateral, regional, and unilateral trade agreements because they have only reported 2 years of annual GDP performance as a member nation of the WTO to the World Bank. Tajikistan's annual GDP mean performance shifted between the two time periods measured 224%, and its annual GDP mean performance increased by 13.96. There is a clear correlation between annual GDP mean performance and membership in the WTO for both Georgia and Moldova. Georgia joined the WTO in 2000, and Moldova joined in 2001. Georgia's annual GDP mean performance grew from 1989 to 2001 in comparison to 2002 to 2014 by 188%, and its annual GDP mean performance increased by 13.13. Moldova's annual mean GDP growth grew from 1989 to 2001 in comparison to 2002 to 2014 by 181%, and its annual GDP mean performance increased by 11.31. These statistics and the level of growth are tremendous in comparison to past annual mean GDP performance, and it is clear that membership in the WTO has benefitted these nations' economies. For new member nations, WTO benefits create favorable business environments for other members to conduct business, and it has resulted in positive investment climates for new members (Lee & Kolesnikova, 2008). This has been especially true for member nations that have substantial natural resources and developed industries within them. There is a negative effect initially on regional trading partners, but the ultimate effect can be seen in the economic growth resulting in increased annual GDP mean performance and secondary effects like improved legal systems within nations and increased competition in specific sectors. The nations with the best performing annual GDP mean performance from 2002 to 2014 were then extracted from the 162 nations measured, and there performance was then compared to their annual GDP mean performance from 1989 to 2001.

A comparison 10 countries with the best annual GDP mean performance from 2002 to 2014 was compared to their annual GDP mean performance from 1989 to 2001.

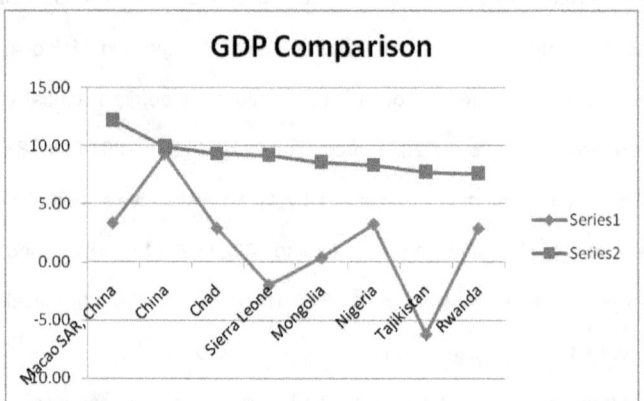

In the above chart, Series 1 represents the annual GDP mean performance from 1989 to 2001 of the top performing countries from this time period, and Series 2 represents the annual GDP mean performance of the same nations from 2002 to 2014. The 3 nations with the largest percentage change from 2002 to 2014 in comparison to 1989 to 2001 were Mongolia, Sierra Leone, and Macao, SAR, China. The entire group of nations showed strong annual GDP mean performance gains when comparing the annual GDP mean performance data from 2002 to 2014 against the annual GDP mean performance data from 1989 to 2001. The entire group's annual GDP mean performance increased 433% from 1989 to 2001 to the 2002 to 2014 time period. It is clear from the growth of the above nations in the comparative time periods that the Trade Facilitation Agreement Facility that was launched in 2013 and other previous measures have positively impacted the growth of developing economies (Akhtar, 2014). The WTO's support and increased multilateral trading opportunities for developing nations will continue to benefit free trade and boost the GDPs of developing economies throughout the world. These countries will most likely continue to face challenges at the national level in the future in relation to legislation, but the benefits of free trade will continue to increase standard of living within these nations and increase access to markets throughout the world. This will ultimately continue to raise economic standards within these nations, and force countries to remove bureaucratic administrative burdens in relation to trade to increase global access to markets. Mongolia, Sierra Leone, and Macao, SAR, China showed the largest percentage increase of annual GDP mean performance between 1989 to 2001 and 2002 to 2014. Mongolia's annual GDP mean performance increased 2,118%, and its annual GDP mean performance increased by 8.19. Sierra Leone's annual GDP mean performance increased by 560%, and its annual GDP mean performance increased by 11.17. Macao, SAR, China's annual GDP mean performance increased by 264%, and its annual GDP mean performance increased by 8.87. Qatar and Cambodia were not considered in this analysis because they failed to report the necessary annual data from 1989 to 2001 required for this study. Mongolia joined the WTO in 1997, and it is clear that the nation's economy has benefitted from its WTO membership and other trade partnerships. Sierra Leone has been a WTO member since 1995, and it became a GATT member in 1961. It is clear that some of the initiatives put forth by the WTO, like the Trade Facilitation Agreement Facility that began in 2013, in conjunction with bilateral, regional, and unilateral trades agreements have had a remarkable impact and reversed the poor economic performance of the nation from 1989 to 2001 in comparison to 2002 to 2014. Macao, SAR, China has been a WTO member since 1995, and it became a GATT member in 1991. Its astonishing annual GDP mean performance growth over the period is not surprising in consideration of China's GDP data reported to the World Bank over the same period and geographic location. The performance of nations like Mongolia, Sierra Leone, and Macao, SAR, China are a great example of how WTO membership can benefit nations and regions, and it shows WTO's policies and other international trade agreements are directly improving economic performance in member nations. The nations with the worst performing annual GDP mean performance from 2002 to 2014 were then extracted from the 162 nations measured, and there performance was then compared to their annual GDP mean performance from 1989 to 2001.

A comparison 10 countries with the worst annual GDP mean performance from 2002 to 2014  was compared to their annual GDP mean performance from 1989 to 2001.

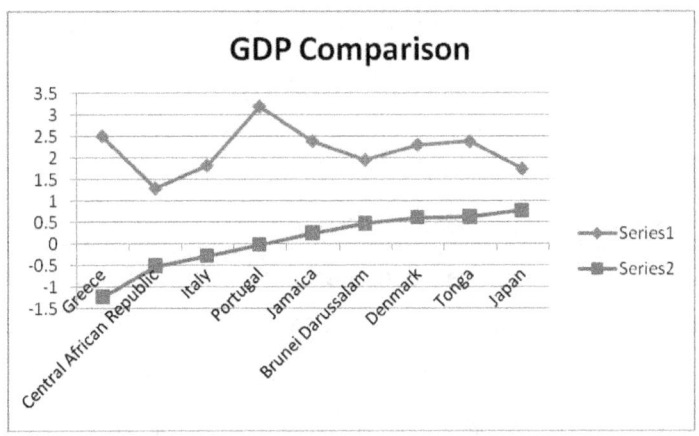

In the above chart, Series 1 represents the annual GDP mean performance from 1989

to 2001 of the worst performing countries from this time period, and Series 2 represents

the annual GDP mean performance of the same nations from 2002 to 2014. The 3

nations with the largest percentage change from 2002 to 2014 in comparison to 1989 to

2001 were Greece, the Central African Republic, and Italy. The entire group of nations

showed low annual GDP mean performance gains when compared to their annual GDP

mean performance data from 1989 to 2001. Croatia was not considered in this analysis

as a result of not reporting an adequate amount of data from 1989 to 2001 to meet the

criteria set forth in this study. Often, countries suffering from economic downturns will

implement austerity measures in an attempt to reduce national debt and boost national

economics (Jadhav et al., 2013). This typically results in the elimination of social

services, government programs, and the reduction of grants to private sector projects

considered to be dispensable by policymakers currently holding office. Economic

downturns for national economies result in increased unemployment rates and poor

GDP growth, which essentially forces governments to adopt austerity measures to survive among economic crises. There has been significant research out of the Eurozone supporting the adoption of austerity measures to quickly remedy economic downturns, which was seen specifically seen in Greece and Spain when both nations reported unemployment rates higher than 25% in the first half of 2013. Unfortunately, there is a great deal of evidence that suggests that austerity programs are incorrectly implemented by policymakers and that the effect of austerity measures taken in economic crises takes a great deal longer than a single political cycle. Many economists also believe that the current austerity measures that are accepted by most governments lead to future recessions and typically lead to an increased debt-to-GDP ratio higher than nations previously experienced prior to austerity measures being implemented. Nations suffering from economic problems should focus on long-term solutions for long-term economic growth that are driven by quality-improving innovations that highlight the importance of technological integration. The downside to this approach is that it has the potential for income inequality because it rewards people with education at the cost of the less educated, especially in developed economies. The performance of Greece, the Central African Republic, and Italy show a large decrease in economic growth and failing austerity measures implemented by policymakers within the nations. The entire group showed an annual GDP mean performance loss of .94 or 94% from the 1989 to 2001 period in comparison to the 2002 to 2014 period. Greece showed an annual GDP mean performance loss of 150%, and its annual GDP mean performance decreased by 3.73. The Central African Republic showed an annual GDP mean performance loss of 140%, and its annual GDP mean performance decreased by

1.81. Italy showed an annual showed an annual GDP mean performance loss 116%, and its annual GDP mean performance decreased by 2.11. It is clear that WTO membership is not benefiting these nations, and they have not properly diversified their economies and adopted policies that support innovation within their nations. All of these nations debt-to-GDP ratios will most likely continue to increase and the inevitability of forthcoming recessions and, possibly, depression is likely. To improve their economic growth, nations showing poor annual GDP mean performance from the 2002 to 2014 in comparison to their annual GDP mean performance from 1989 to 2002 should adopt responsible austerity measures and analyze their current bilateral, regional, and unilateral trade agreements. Greece joined the WTO in 1995, and it has been a GATT member since 1950. It is clear that the measures taken by the WTO to boost developing economies has negatively impacted Greece in conjunction with its national policymaking, and it should be reanalyzing its membership in the WTO and the European Union, which was formed in 1993, because the economic benefits seen as being a member nation to both organizations are clearly not beneficial to its economy. The Central African Republic became a member nation of the WTO in 1995, and it joined GATT in 1963. The Central African Republic is one of the world's least developed nations, and it is clear that WTO membership and GATT membership can be said to have had little impact on the nation's economic development. The nation is clearly suffering from poor policymaking, infrastructure, and trade partnerships leading to sustainable economic growth and investment. Italy became a WTO member in 1995, and a GATT member in 1950. Its economic problems are similar to Greece's, and it should be reviewing its decision to being a member to the WTO and the European Union. It should also be reviewing it bilateral, regional, and unilateral trade agreements.

The top 10 countries with the largest positive annual GDP mean performance shift between 1989 to 2001 and 2002 to 2014 are shown in the graph below.

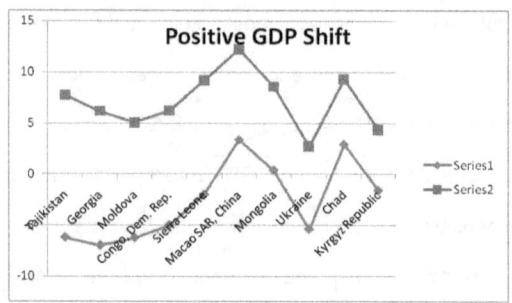

In the above chart, Series 1 represents the annual GDP mean performance from 1989 to 2001 of the WTO member nations who had the largest positive annual GDP mean performance shift in comparison to the annual GDP mean performance reported in Series 2, which represents the annual GDP mean performance of the same nations from 2002 to 2014. The information from this data is extremely positive for the economic growth and citizens of the nations listed. Tajikistan joined the WTO in 2013, Georgia joined the WTO in 2000, the Republic of Moldova joined the WTO in 2001, the Democratic Republic of the Congo joined the WTO in 1997, Sierra Leone joined the WTO in 1995 and was a GATT member since 1961, Macao SAR, China joined in 1995 and was a GATT member since 1991, Mongolia joined the WTO in 1997, the Ukraine joined the WTO in 2008, Chad joined the WTO in 1996 and was a GATT member since 1963, and the Kyrgyz Republic joined the WTO in 1998. Between the two periods,

Tajikistan's annual GDP mean performance increased by 13.97, Georgia's annual GDP mean performance increased by 13.13, Moldova's annual GDP mean performance increased by 11.31, the Democratic Republic of the Congo's annual GDP mean performance increased by 11.21, Sierra Leone's annual GDP mean performance increased by 11.17, Macao SAR, China's annual GDP mean performance increased by 8.87, Mongolia's annual GDP mean performance increased by 8.19, Ukraine's annual GDP mean performance increased by 8.06, Chad's annual GDP mean performance increased by 6.39, and Kyrgyz Republic's annual GDP mean performance increased by 5.95. The commonality among all of these nations is serious economic improvement between the two time periods measured. It is clear that WTO membership can be said to be working for most of these nations in conjunction with national policymaking in relation to their bilateral, regional, and unilateral trade agreements. Tajikistan and the Ukraine are the newest members of the above group, and it is not clear from this data which has benefitted them more, their WTO membership or their former bilateral, regional, and unilateral trade agreements, because they have reported less economic data as WTO members in comparison to other members who have shown drastic economic performance changes within this group. It is clear that the WTO's focus on assisting developing nations has clearly benefitted the other members of the group and that Macao SAR, China has clearly increased its annual GDP mean performance over the two time periods measured because of East Asian Regional success over the same time period, specifically the People's Republic of China. Many economists continue question the effectiveness of WTO membership, and they claim the WTO fails in promoting trade (Subramanian & Wei, 2007). This, however, is untrue, and the WTO has been shown by many economic studies to have increased trade throughout the world by over 120%. Studies have also shown that WTO membership helps nations develop bilateral, regional, and unilateral trade networks through its trade promotion, but this has come at a cost, specifically to developed countries, who have not seen as much economic in comparison WTO members who are considered developing nations.

The top 10 countries with the largest negative annual GDP mean performance loss between 1989 to 2001 and 2002 to 2014 are shown in the graph below.

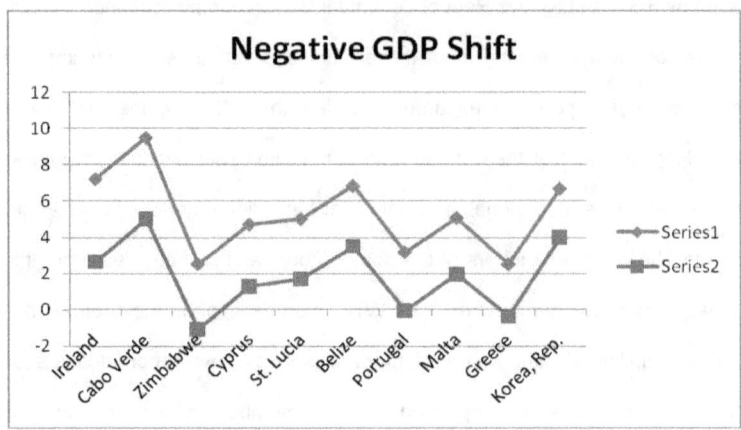

In the above chart, Series 1 represents the annual GDP mean performance from 1989 to 2001 of the WTO member nations who have had the largest negative annual GDP mean performance shift in comparison to the annual GDP mean performance reported in Series 2, which represents the annual GDP mean performance of the same nations from 2002 to 2014. The information from this data is extremely negative for the economic growth and citizens of the nations listed, and it should act as a signal to the policymakers who have implemented austerity measures in some of these countries and economists within these countries who advise policymakers regarding economic policy and trade memberships. Ireland joined the WTO in 1995 and has been a GATT member since 1967, Cabo Verde joined the WTO in 2008, and Zimbabwe joined the WTO in 1995 and has been a GATT member since 1947, Cyprus joined the WTO in 1995 and has been a GATT member since 1963, Saint Lucia has been a WTO member since 1995 and has been a GATT since 1993, Belize has been a WTO member since 1995 and has been a GATT member since 1983, Portugal joined the WTO in 1995 and has been a GATT member since 1962, Malta joined the WTO in 1995 and has been a GATT member since 1964, Greece joined the WTO in 1995 and has been a GATT member since 1950, and the Republic of Korea joined the WTO in 1995 and has been a GATT member since 1967. Between the two periods, Ireland's annual GDP mean performance decreased by 4.58, Cabo Verde's annual GDP mean performance decreased by 4.47, Zimbabwe's annual GDP performance decreased by 3.59, Cyprus's annual GDP performance decreased by 3.41, Saint Lucia's annual GDP performance decreased by 3.41, Belize's annual GDP performance decreased by 3.42, Portugal's annual GDP performance decreased by 3.22, Malta's annual GDP performance decreased by 3.12, Greece's annual GDP performance decreased by 2.87, and the Republic of Korea's annual GDP performance decreased by 2.68. With the exception of Cabo Verde in this group, there is an alarming trend that shows long time members of the WTO, who were formerly GATT members, economies are currently suffering. This is clearly the result of many world economic factors, but policymakers and economists advising them within these nations should be extremely cautious in continuing their current membership in trade organizations and continuing trade partnerships. For these nations, it can be said that the economic benefits previously brought to them as members of GATT, the WTO, and, for some, the European Union are no longer being seen. Some economists have shown that both GATT and the WTO have not had a dramatic effect on trade, and that bilateral trading partnerships and Generalized System of Preferences in trade have a more measurable effect on national economies (Rose, 2004). Although it is difficult to say whether WTO has had an effect on world trade, it is commonly accepted that it has had a positive effect on trade relations and encouraged world trade that may not have existed without the organization. It is clear that the WTO has had little effected on forcing developing countries to alter trade significantly, and its focus on assisting to promote developing economies throughout has left many long-time members to the organization economies behind, which has caused some of the European Union members nations, who are also WTO member nations, economies to contract and resulted in the adoption of austerity measures.

## Conclusion

The comparative analysis of the two time periods annual GDP mean performance for all 162 member nations of the WTO from the time period 1989 to 2001 against the time period 2002-2014 shows a radical change in annual GDP mean performance for many countries. It can be said with certainty that many WTO member nations are benefitting from current WTO promotion of free trade and the bilateral, unilateral, and regional trade networks their governments have negotiated. It can also be said with certitude that many long-time WTO and GATT members are not currently benefitting economically as they once had from the historically beneficial trade networks. It is clear that many developed nations economies have suffered under WTO's trade policies and promotion of developed nations over the last 20 years has led to some substantial positive annual GDP mean performance by newer members to the WTO.

It can be definitively concluded the annual GDP mean performance for all member nations increased by 29% between the two time periods measured. This measurement shows that the WTO's policies regarding free trade and the addition of new members over the two time periods has benefitted world trade as a whole, specifically for the 162 member nations of the WTO. The second measurement analyzing the top annual GDP mean performance from the 1989 to 2001 time period against their annual GDP mean performance from 2002 to 2014 shows a decrease of 21% or a decrease in annual GDP mean performance by 1.57 by the WTO nations in the group. Out of the entire group, we see a trend of longtime WTO members economically suffering.

| Country Name | Year of Acceptance | GDP Mean 1989-2001 | GDP Mean 2002-2014 | GDP Shift |
|---|---|---|---|---|
| Cabo Verde | 2008 | 9.504301006 | 5.033380159 | -4.470920847 |
| China | 2001 | 9.311780299 | 9.930601164 | 0.618820865 |
| Mozambique | 1992 | 7.392397747 | 7.515159205 | 0.122761458 |
| Vietnam | 2007 | 7.271912916 | 6.36823974 | -0.903873176 |
| Ireland | 1967 | 7.216977262 | 2.641640315 | -4.575336947 |
| Singapore | 1973 | 7.010095099 | 5.928084078 | -1.082011021 |
| Malaysia | 1957 | 6.993458832 | 5.1843119 | -1.809146932 |
| Myanmar | 1948 | 6.921814059 | *not enough data* | *not enough data* |
| Belize | 1983 | 6.836949903 | 3.512692585 | -3.324257318 |
| Lao PDR | 2013 | 6.806081578 | 7.505378426 | 0.699296848 |
| | **1984.9** | **7.52657687** | **5.957720841** | **-1.568856029** |

This data shows that these nations are not benefitting from trade partnerships created through the WTO, and they have failed to adequately create innovation within their economies necessary to be competitive in the global marketplace when adopting austerity measures. It also shows that these economies have not properly diversified themselves, and they are suffering from cyclical changes in the global economy, which is negatively impacting their annual GDP mean performance. Finally, it shows that these nations have not set up the necessary bilateral, regional, and unilateral trade networks to be economically successful as a nation in today's global trade network. For Ireland, it is clear that being a member of the European Union may be having negative effects on its economic growth as a nation. This is beyond the scope of this analysis, but the data does show that the present trading partnerships the nation has are not benefitting it economically in the same manner as it once did.

The third measurement analyzing the worst annual GDP mean performance from the 1989 to 2001 time period against the their annual GDP mean performance from the 2002 to 2014, which shows an increase of 243% or an increase in annual GDP mean performance by 9.21 by the WTO nations in the group.

| Country Name | Year of Acceptance | GDP Mean 1989-2001 | GDP Mean 2002-2014 | GDP Shift |
|---|---|---|---|---|
| Georgia | 2000 | -6.980494665 | 6.151998314 | 13.1324929 |
| Moldova | 2001 | -6.251362832 | 5.057245246 | 11.3086080 |
| Tajikistan | 2013 | -6.215384727 | 7.753788504 | 13.9691732 |
| Ukraine | 2008 | -5.380148215 | 2.684614815 | 8.06476303 |
| Congo, Dem. Rep. | 1997 | -4.997698797 | 6.208615572 | 11.2063143 |
| Russian Federation | 2012 | -2.830654114 | 4.143228731 | 6.97388284 |
| Sierra Leone | 1961 | -1.996820231 | 9.175773867 | 11.1725941 |

| | | | | |
|---|---|---|---|---|
| gyz Republic | 1998 | -1.591536826 | 4.362538586 | 5.954075412 |
| Burundi | 1965 | -0.906530597 | 3.761180688 | 4.667711285 |
| Cuba | 1948 | -0.782850534 | 4.831512942 | 5.614363476 |
| | **1990.3** | **-3.793348154** | **5.413049727** | **9.20639788** |

This annual GDP mean performance shift is for some members of this group is clearly the result of the WTO's focusing on opening up developing economies to the world markets to increase trade, and this has resulted in a positive shift in annual GDP mean performance of these nations between the 1989 to 2001 time period in comparison to the 2002 to the 2014 time period. It is also clear that the austerity measures implemented at a national level during the economic contractions experienced by these nations during the 1989 to 2001 time period where effective in boosting national economies between the 2002 to 2014 time period. These nations have also clearly established the necessary bilateral, regional, and unilateral trade networks necessary to increase access to global markets in the twenty-first century in conjunction with their membership in the WTO. For the nations among the group that recently joined the WTO, Tajikistan, the Russian Federation, and Ukraine, it is difficult to say with certainty if the annual GDP mean performance success that they experienced between 2002 to 2014 time was a result of WTO membership. Acceptance to the WTO in conjunction with establishing bilateral, regional, and unilateral trade partnerships is the most likely factor in increasing annual GDP mean performance of these nations, so the result of the positive shift of annual GDP mean performance is most likely a combination of the simultaneous effect of both trade partnerships and WTO memberships. An examination of each country's economic reforms implemented during the 1989 to 2001 time period in comparison to their annual GDP mean performance in the 2002 to 2014 time period would have to be analyzed to say with complete certainty, which is beyond the scope of this study.    An examination of some of the other nations that are part of the group whose membership in the organization is more than 50 years old, Cuba, Sierra Leone, and Burundi, suggests that some of the economic hardships experienced by these nations between the 1989 to 2002 time period in relation  to annual GDP mean performance could have been cyclical, but it is more likely that they are showing annual GDP mean performance increases directly as a result of increased trade and the WTO's promotion of free trade throughout the world in combination with the WTO's focus on opening up developing economies to increased trade opportunities.

The fourth measurement analyzed the best annual GDP mean performance from the 2002 to 2014 time period against the annual GDP mean performance of the same WTO members from 1989 to 2002 time period, and it shows an increase of 433% or an increase in annual GDP mean performance by 7.54 by the WTO nations in the group.

| Country Name | Year of Acceptance | GDP Mean 1989-2001 | GDP Mean 2002-2014 | GDP Shift |
|---|---|---|---|---|
| Macao SAR, China | 1991 | 3.361538458 | 12.2342128 | 8.872674344 |
| Qatar | 1994 | *not enough data* | 12.13820867 | *not enough data* |
| China | 2001 | 9.311780299 | 9.930601164 | 0.618820865 |
| Chad | 1963 | 2.909345526 | 9.298498454 | 6.389152928 |
| Sierra Leone | 1961 | -1.996820231 | 9.175773867 | 11.1725941 |
| Mongolia | 1997 | 0.38666376 | 8.576687919 | 8.19002416 |
| Nigeria | 1960 | 3.265903504 | 8.328758113 | 5.062854608 |
| Cambodia | 2004 | *not enough data* | 7.799371353 | *not enough data* |
| Tajikistan | 2013 | -6.215384727 | 7.753788504 | 13.96917323 |
| Rwanda | 1966 | 2.908670222 | 7.592289805 | 4.683619583 |
| **1985** | | **1.741462101** | **9.282819065** | **7.541356964** |

This data shows many members who joined the WTO in the 1990s and newer members who have recently been accepted to the organization have benefitted significantly to increased access to global markets. It is clear that WTO membership and bilateral, regional, and unilateral trade networks that have been put in place at the national level are having a direct impact of positive annual GDP mean shift. The intertwined global network of trade has clearly increased access to new markets for these nations to sell manufactured goods and raw materials needed to produce these goods. Individuals within these nations are clearly seeing the benefit at the local level of their nations being members of the WTO with increased standards of living, improved legislation regarding trade, and better employment opportunities. The WTO's promotion of trade networks for developing nations has changed the lives of millions of individuals within these nations, and it is clear from their annual GDP mean performance that WTO membership has continued to assist in the development of wealth within most of these nations that began previously to the 1989 to 2001 time period and continued into the 2002 to 2014 time period, specifically the Asian nations. For other nations in the group, the WTO has assisted in helping in ending economic contractions and stagnant economic development between the 1989 to 2001 time period in comparison to the 2002 to 2014 time period.

The fifth measurement analyzed the worst annual GDP mean performance from WTO member nations from the 2002 to 2014 time period against the annual GDP mean performance of the same WTO members from 1989 to 2002 time period, and it shows a decrease annual GDP mean performance of 93% or a decrease in the annual GDP mean performance by 2.04 by the WTO nations in the group.

| Country Name | Year of Acceptance | GDP Mean 1989-2001 | GDP Mean 2002-2014 | GDP Shift |
|---|---|---|---|---|

| | | | | |
|---|---|---|---|---|
| Greece | 1950 | 2.497079815 | -1.239518088 | -3.736597903 |
| Central African Republic | 1963 | 1.297202206 | -0.519661276 | -1.816863482 |
| Italy | 1950 | 1.824300893 | -0.287251327 | -2.11155222 |
| Portugal | 1962 | 3.183605039 | -0.031230692 | -3.214835731 |
| Jamaica | 1963 | 2.384664038 | 0.239799255 | -2.144864783 |
| Brunei Darussalam | 1993 | 1.949438381 | 0.458505288 | -1.490933093 |
| Denmark | 1950 | 2.296494483 | 0.599189118 | -1.697305365 |
| Tonga | 2007 | 2.374305096 | 0.614594398 | -1.759710698 |
| Croatia | 2000 | *not enough data* | 0.720533739 | *not enough data* |
| Japan | 1955 | 1.744543148 | 0.770255353 | -0.974287795 |
| | **1969.3** | **2.172403678** | **0.132521577** | **-2.039882101** |

An analysis of this group of WTO nations with the worst annual GDP mean performance during the 2002 to 2014 time period is startling. The majority of nations shown above are longtime WTO members, and 5 of the nations listed are EU members. This data suggests that, despite increasing and promoting world trade, WTO membership does not necessarily result in strong annual GDP mean performance. For Greece, Italy, Portugal, Denmark, and Croatia, it can also be said that EU membership does not necessarily lead to strong annual GDP mean performance or increased access to trade networks that benefit annual GDP mean performance. All nations listed above have suffered drastic economic contractions in comparison to the overall performance of other WTO members during the 2002 to 2014 period, and they must reevaluate their WTO membership and other trade partnerships. It is clear that unemployment rates within these nations can be said to be high, the standard of living is decreasing, and austerity measures must be underway to avoid further economic contractions. The goal of these nations should be to implement austerity measures that focus on long-term growth of the nation that incorporate technology and supports innovation within its society. These nations should also consider establishing new bilateral, regional, and unilateral trade partnerships, and the EU member nations listed above should be reexamining the benefit derived from their membership in the EU or lack thereof.

The sixth measurement analyzed the largest positive annual GDP mean performance shift by WTO member nations from the 1989 to 2001 time period in comparison to the 2002 to 2014 time period, and the seventh measurement analyzed the largest negative annual GDP mean performance shift by WTO member nations from the 1989 to 2001 time period in comparison to the 2002 to 2014 time period.

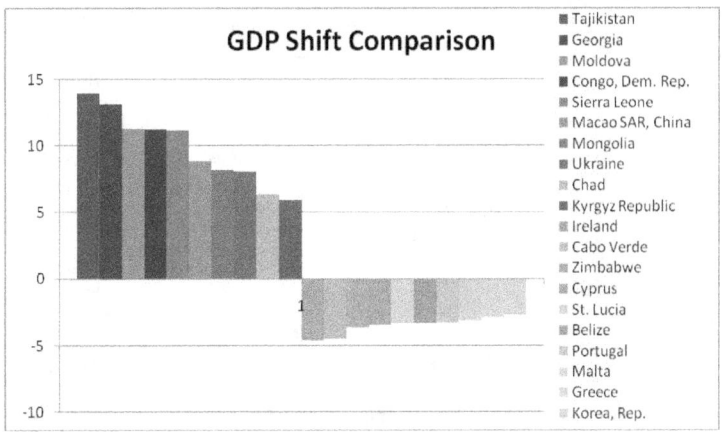

The information received from this analysis displayed on the above chart shows a dramatic difference in the effectiveness of the WTO promotion of developing economies versus developed, and the lack of benefit derived by many longtime WTO members. One could easily argue that there is an imbalance of support by the organization for developed nations, and they are suffering from being WTO members as it pertains to the annual GDP mean performances in comparison to the 1989 to 2001 time period and the 2002 to 2014 time period. The chart also shows substantial growth by newer members to the WTO, and the obvious benefit to their economies displayed in their annual GDP mean performance as a result of increased access to the global markets through the WTO and other trade partnerships.

| Country Name | Year of Acceptance | Positive GDP of Gains Between 1989-2001 and 2002-2014 | Country Name | Year of Acceptance | Negative GDP of Losses Between 1989-2001 and 2002-2014 |
|---|---|---|---|---|---|
| Tajikistan | 2013 | 13.97 | Ireland | 1967 | -4.58 |
| Georgia | 2000 | 13.13 | Cabo Verde | 2008 | -4.47 |
| Moldova | 2001 | 11.31 | Zimbabwe | 1948 | -3.59 |
| Congo, Dem. Rep. | 1997 | 11.21 | Cyprus | 1963 | -3.41 |
| Sierra Leone | 1961 | 11.17 | St. Lucia | 1993 | -3.33 |
| Macao SAR, China | 1991 | 8.87 | Belize | 1983 | -3.32 |
| Mongolia | 1997 | 8.19 | Portugal | 1962 | -3.22 |
| Ukraine | 2008 | 8.06 | Malta | 1964 | -3.13 |
| Chad | 1963 | 6.39 | Greece | 1950 | -2.87 |
| Kyrgyz Republic | 1998 | 5.95 | Korea, Rep. | 1967 | -2.68 |
| | **1992.9** | **9.825** | | **1970.5** | **-3.46** |

The sixth measurement, displayed on the left, shows a positive annual GDP mean performance shift by the nations. The commonality among these nations is that they are newer members of the WTO in comparison the nations analyzed in the seventh measurement. Geographically, the majority of these nations are in Eastern Europe or Asia. They show an average date of acceptance to the WTO in 1993, and they showed an average annual GDP mean positive performance shift between 1989 to 2001 in comparison to 2002 to 2014 of 9.83. The seventh measurement, displayed on the right, shows a negative performance shift by the nations. The commonality among these nations are that they are older members of the WTO in comparison to the nations analyzed in the sixth measurement, the majority are islands, and 5 of the nations are members of the EU. The first commonality shows that long-term WTO membership does not necessarily benefit nations in relation to trade in the twenty-first century, which suggests that nations constantly must work to establish and maintain bilateral, regional, and unilateral trade partnerships outside of the WTO. This data also suggests that small island nations are vulnerable to economic fluctuations as a result of a lack of resources and diversification among economic sectors within their nations. This also shows that smaller nations can potentially be economically ostracized when they are not included large trade agreements, like the Trans-Pacific Partnership and the Trans-Atlantic Trade and Investment Partnership, because of the size of their national economies. Finally, this data shows that nearly 20% of EU member countries are suffering in relation to annual GDP mean performance from the 1989 to 2001 time period in comparison to the 2002 to 2014 time period. This is alarming in consideration of the fact that the EU is one of the world's largest economies, and this information suggests that not all EU members benefit economically from EU membership.

This study shows that free trade has increased throughout the world because of the WTO's promotion of it and other trade networks established between nations. Free trade has benefitted many that are WTO member nations that are considered developing economies and caused other WTO member nations that are considered developed economies to contract. It cannot be said that the WTO's focus on developing economies has been bad specifically for developed economies in relation to the data reviewed in this study, so the initial hypothesis in this study is incorrect. China's entrance as well as other newer members of the WTO have had a positive overall effect on the annual GDP mean performance of the 162 WTO member nations, which can be seen in the increase of the annual GDP mean performance overall of the 162 member nations by 29% from the 1989 to 2001 time period in comparison to the 2002 to 2014 time period. This investigation has clearly shown that many longtime member nations of the WTO are suffering economically, specifically smaller economies, island nations, and nations that are members of the EU. It cannot be specifically said that this is a result of WTO's current policies or the entrance of large developing economies to the WTO. It is, however, clear that the benefits seen between the two time periods measured are not being experienced by all member nations of the WTO. Many of the members who are presently suffering from poor annual GDP mean performance are longtime members of the WTO, and some are conjunctively members of the EU.

## Reference Citations

Akhtar, S. (2014). Asia-Pacific ready to lead and shape sustainable trade and development, *International Trade Forum*, 3(1), p. 16.

Baldwin, R. (2016). The World Trade Organization and the Future of Multilateralism, *The Journal of Economic Perspectives*, 30(1), p. 96-115.

Beattie, A. (2016). The Dark Side Of The WTO. Retrieved online from: http://www.investopedia.com/articles/economics/dark-side-of-the-wto.asp?o=40186&l=dir&qsrc=999&qo=investopediaSiteSearch.

European Union (2016). Official Website of the European Union. Retrieved online from: http://europa.eu/index_en.htm.

Heakal, R. (2016). What Is The World Trade Organization? Retrieved online from: http://www.investopedia.com/articles/03/040203.asp?o=40186&l=dir&qsrc=999&qo=investopediaSiteSearch.

Investopedia (2016). What is GDP and why is it so important to economists and investors? Retrieve online from: http://www.investopedia.com/ask/answers/199.asp.

Jadhav, A., Neelankavil, J., and Andrews, D. (2013). Determinants of GDP Growth and the Impact of Austerity, *Journal of Applied Business and Economics*, 15(1), p. 15-29.

Lee, C.Y. & Kolesnikova, E. (2008). Russia's Accession of WTO Membership and Its Implications on the Russian Economy, *Journal of Global Business Management*, 6(1), p. 137-147.

Porter, R. (2015). The World Trade Organization at Twenty, *The Brown Journal of World Affairs*, 12(2), p. 103-116.

Rose, A. (2004). Do We Really Know that the WTO Increases Trade?, *The American Economic Review*, 94(1), p. 98-114.

Subramanian, A. & Wei, S. (2007). The WTO promotes trade, strongly but unevenly, *Journal of International Economics*, 72(1), p. 151-175.

The World Bank Group. Data. Retrieved online from: http://data.worldbank.org/.

World Trade Organization (2016). Members and Observers. Retrieved online from: https://www.wto.org/english/thewto_e/whatis_e/tif_e/org6_e.htm.

www.ingramcontent.com/pod-product-compliance
Lightning Source LLC
Chambersburg PA
CBHW070402190526
45169CB00003B/1072